A Journey into My Mind, Body and Soul

Sabrina Souviron Gumucio

BookLeaf Publishing

India | USA | UK

A Journey into My Mind, Body and Soul

© 2022 Sabrina Souviron Gumucio

Presentation by *BookLeaf Publishing*

Web: www.bookleafpub.com

E-mail: info@bookleafpub.com

ISBN: 9789357611602

First edition 2022

To my parents, thank you for being in my
corner and supporting my dreams.

I also dedicate this to anyone who is struggling
to fight the demons in their head.

There is always light and you are never alone.

ACKNOWLEDGEMENT

I would like to express my deepest gratitude to Camila Uriona Crespo. As a fellow poet, she took the time to carefully review my poems and taught me how to be a better writer. Her continuous support was instrumental in allowing me to find my creative voice.

I would also like to thank the universe for putting these challenges in my path. If I hadn't gone through the pain, I wouldn't be able to write this book nor would I be the strong, resilient woman I am today.

The Illusion of Perfection

"Not good enough", "Average", "Failure",
those words hit you like a gut punch to the chest,
you have to be the best,
it is the only stairway to satisfaction,
no one can hurt or judge you if you're king
or queen of the castle.

People complimenting and congratulating you
for being number one,
the glow of exhilaration from being celebrated,
accepted by others
gives you permission to look at yourself
with admiration of what you've done,
but it's all just a pretty illusion,
a safety net to disguise the truth.

The reality is there is no top of the castle,
you strive to climb up an endless rope
for a temporary spark of achievement,
when the light goes out
you find yourself at the bottom again,
frustrated and burned out.

The Cycle of Bullying

ASHAMED, DEFENCELESS, ENRAGED!
That's what I feel with his brutal attacks.
The beatings sting like a hundred icy lashes
covering up daily bruises,
an average day for me,
what wounds and hurts me the most are his
venomous insults.

Every day at the school gates
I see a dad embrace his son lovingly,
why does he get an adoring father?
Mine welcomes me with smacks of violence
and agony,
seeing the dad I should have...
It makes my blood BOIL!

I'll even the score, let him have his doting dad,
in exchange he gets to feel unbearable suffering,
I'll taunt him, torment him, put him down,
let's see if he can survive my ANGUISH and
PAIN!

HUMILIATED, OUTCASTED, AFRAID!
Every day at school is a nightmare,
I quiver in fear
never knowing what punishment awaits me,

will he seize my lunch
that my dad kindly made me?
or spread false rumours that leave me
embarrassed and isolated?

I wonder what crime I committed to deserve
such cruelty,
as his kickings and poundings
always end up with me lying on the ground,
feeling like an injured animal
savagely mauled by lions.
Sick of being so weak, pathetic and vulnerable,

I know now for sure
my real self will never fit in,
the new boy in my class will be my target,
he's fresh meat,
the perfect prey to assert my power,
I will NOT be at the bottom of the food chain!

ANXIOUS, HATED, DEGRADED!
Living in terror ever since I've moved here,
his nasty name-calling and menacing threats
is like a gut-punch to my self-esteem,
the violent abuse follows me home as he
harasses me online.

Why use me as a punching bag
to take his frustrations out on?

All I've been to him is kind.
I tried to show him empathy
when I saw him curled up on the floor
all he did was throw it back at me,
cutting down my confidence with rude words.

I'll report the abuse,
tell someone to put an end to all this misery,
spreading hate and viciousness
is never the answer,
LOVE and KINDNESS is the first step
to healing,
manipulation and malice don't control me
anymore.

I refuse to continue this cycle of bullying!

The Blows of Rejection

My first day of school,
excited to make new friends,
I say goodbye to my mum and dad, and rush in,
my teachers are nice,
I can't wait to meet my new friends!

It's break time! Yay!
Who will be my new best friend?
I run to the playground, eagerly looking around,
deciding who I should talk to first,

I see a group of three girls who I sat next to
in class,
I walk up to them with a kind smile and say hi,
they look at me with disappointment
in their eyes and tell me "You're weird."

"We don't want to be friends with you."

With a heavy heart, I walk away from them,
all the joy I had, replaced with sadness
and confusion.
I wonder what is so wrong with me
they couldn't give me a chance,
I feel like an ugly duckling
for the first time ever...

My first boyfriend, how exciting!
It's been three months
and things couldn't be any better,
we've gotten closer
and started making plans about our future,

he makes me laugh and is incredibly charming,
he's so kind and sincere,
my heart wants to explode,
and he's so devoted to me.

I receive a text from him… WHAT?
He broke up with me!
He says it's him and not me.
What does that even mean?
My heart is broken into a million pieces,
I sob uncontrollably,
I could fill a hundred jars with my tears.
How will I ever go on?

Not even a day has gone by
and he's already moved on,
posting selfies with his new girlfriend,
saying she's "the one",
I gave him one hundred percent
of my love and commitment.
How could he do this?...

My first dream job, I can see it in my grasp,
just one more interview and then I will celebrate,
I'm in the final three,
this will be a walk in the park,

Surely no one could be a better candidate
than me,
I know the industry inside out,
I've researched the company thoroughly.
What more do I need to prove?

The interviewer calls my name,
I confidently introduce myself,
I sit down and suddenly feel a ripple of nerves
shiver through my body,
my hands are sweaty, my throat becomes sore
and my thoughts go blank like a train
derailed from the tracks.

I didn't get the job…
What the hell came over me?
Panic and fear possessed me,
leaving me frozen as an iceberg.
How am I supposed to get anywhere
if my emotions betray me?
My confidence is shattered
like a brick thrown through a window…

Party Phobia

My heart drops suddenly at the question,
"Will you come to my birthday party
next Saturday?"
For my friend it's a fun occasion,
for me a dreaded nightmare.

I try to think of any excuse
of why I can't go
but alas none come to mind,
I feign a happy smile and reply,
"Of course. Looking forward to it."
But it's all a fake performance.

So many strangers will be at the party…
Why did I say yes?
What if I say something stupid?
What if I do something wrong?
What if they laugh at me?
What if they all hate me?
Worried and stressed,
my stomach feels like it's been tied
into a knot of anxiety.

It's Saturday,
I haven't been able to sleep all week,
a tsunami of what-ifs and questions

overwhelm my mind,
the knot has grown
into a bowling ball of anxiety
making me feel nauseous and sick,

I really can't do this!
Maybe I should cancel-
Crap!
I hear the doorbell… she's here.
As she drives us to the party,
every part of me is screaming not to go,
should I fake an emergency?
No, there's no turning back now.

As I walk in, my heart is pounding
faster and faster every second,
I feel dizzy and light-headed
seeing all these people I don't know,
my friend introduces me
to a group of her colleagues,
my face feels red hot
as I push down the fears and negativity,

I shake their hands,
afraid my sweaty hands will give me away
but shockingly they don't seem to notice.
After a while of talking and exchanging stories,
I start to relax,
all worries and stress fade away,

no more ball nor knot of anxiety.

To my surprise I had so much fun at the party!
Everyone was really friendly and welcoming,
there was no reason to be so nervous,
turns out, the fear was bigger in my head.

A Bouquet of Memories of My Dad

Do you remember the 10th of December 1999?
We spent the day, just you and I,
father and daughter having fun together,
drinking hot chocolate and seeing The
Nutcracker.

Do you remember the countless times
we went to the park?
You would push me on the swings so high
I thought that I could touch the sky.

My favourite time together
was when we would walk home from school,
we'd talk of our days
with your hand holding mine,
I never felt safer with you by my side.

Now you're gone
as if you've vanished into smoke,
one moment I could hear you,
see you and feel your hugs,
the next you became a bouquet of memories
of the life you vibrantly lived.

My life has turned upside down
without you here to encourage and guide me,

I feel as lost as a scared little kid alone
in a big crowded shopping centre.

This unfathomable blow
pierces my heart like an arrow,
I struggle to breathe as it shatters.
As soon as I begin to breathe once more,
I'm stricken all over again with any reminders
of you.

One thing that will never die
is the love that you gave my family and I,
the lessons, the memories, your belief in me
will always be remembered and ingrained in me.

Even though you're not here anymore
I can still see you,
especially in my children's eyes,
I can still hear you in my head,
dreaming of our conversations,
I can still feel you in my heart,
as I tell your stories to my children.

An Unheeded Distress Signal

There once was a shy girl
who just started college,
there she met a boy
who showered her with praises,
he was a master of deceit
who blinded her with custom-made lies
so he could control and possess her like a toy.

The girl saw through his deception,
refusing to be his puppet.
Like a predator, he tried to lure his prey
into his trap with empty sweet talk,
yet over and over again,
the girl said no.

Aggravated, the boy decided to go with a more
aggressive approach,
he cornered her,
degraded her with vile desires to plough her
until she breaks,
he stalked her every day at college,
he even attempted to follow her home.

The girl felt violated and repulsed,
as if his sick fantasies
manifested into cockroaches

that crawled into every layer of her skin,

Always looking over her shoulder,
terrified of what he might do next,
taking as many different routes home,
desperate to escape his pursuit.

She confided in her teacher and a counsellor,
hoping this nightmare would end,
yet all they both said was,
"You're being melodramatic",
"You must have led him on,
given him the wrong impression",
"Boys will be boys",
"There is nothing we can do."

The girl was at a loss,
she was sending a distress signal,
but the powers that be didn't want to hear her.
How was this behaviour normal?
She didn't do anything wrong.
Constantly fearing for her safety,
why was she getting blamed?

How is this right? This was not her fault.

She was never the same,
leaving a permanent mark on her
that she could never scrub off.

The girl isolated herself,
rarely letting anyone in the barrier she created,
afraid to trust again.

Haunted by My Worries, Fears and Obligations

Exhausted,
I am about to drop,
but when I close my eyes
deadlines,
responsibilities,
unpleasant memories
and fears,
rush through my head,
smacking me wide awake.

Exasperated,
four nights in a row of horrifying reminders
forcing my eyes to stay open,
just the moon, my restless demons and I
up here alone again in the dead of night,
while everyone else slumbers below.

The blue light of the TV helps to decompress
and diminish any tension
pushing down my thoughts,
I keep all the lights on,
as if they could shield me from the fear
of seeing the cold, sinister visions.

I listen to soft, calming music
to quiet the anxious voices in my mind,

this is so infuriating!

I'm losing my patience! I need to sleep.
The more I'm awake, alone at night,
the further I descend into madness!
Yet if I go to sleep…
I'm afraid the demons will follow
and turn my dreams into nightmares.

The Awakening of The Snake in My Belly

The snake awakens in my belly,
turning my arms and legs into jelly,
its scaly skin spiralling up
tightening my throat.

The snake hisses in my ear,
its voice making my heart pound in fear.

"You can't do it!
You're mad.
You're better off with regrets
and being sad."

At first, I ignore the voice
and focus on my breathing,
I take a slow deep breath in...
then out...
as I try to wash away this feeling.

"Your friends and family don't care,
they're better off without you!"

Do not try to rattle me,
I know you are untrue.

I close my eyes,
I conjure up a phrase to heal and protect me,

Everything will be alright,
I am loved,
I am worthy,
I deserve happiness.
I am courage,
I will defeat you.

The snake goes back to sleep for now.

Calm waves overcome my soul
wrapped in a velvet blanket of relief.

I have won today.

Will I prevail tomorrow?

Round, Round the Carousel I Go

Round, round the carousel I go,
where does it stop? Nobody knows,
ecstatic with glee
as the horse bounces up and down,
not sure what to expect on this merry-go-round.

Round, round the carousel I go,
when does it stop? Nobody knows,
looking around as I start to feel dizzy,
realising suddenly I'm alone with no one around.

Round, round the carousel I go,
when will this stop? Nobody knows,
this isn't fun anymore!
I'm feeling light-headed and queasy,
I'm sick of feeling worn out, exhausted,
rundown.

Round, round the carousel I go,
how the hell will this end? Nobody knows,
I've lost all control, my life feels like it's inside
out, bewildered, confused
and on the verge of a nervous BREAKDOWN!

Round, round the carousel I go .

Punishment by Fury and Self-Hatred

I slam the door behind me,
a minute of quiet,
then like race cars with the signal to go,
a million feelings from today
race through my mind.

Drained, tense, overwhelmed, anxious,
mortified, panic spin through me,
like clothes in a washing machine.
All these emotions build and build
until it all morphs into a burning ball of fury
and hatred.

Pacing the room back and forth
I try to control the fire within me,
but it continues to spread and grow,
I can feel it,
an explosion is imminent!

If I erupt like a volcano,
I'm afraid who I will hurt
by the flaming hot lava,
the anger has to come out,
I can't contain it any longer!
The only one who deserves to be in pain is me,
instead of raging out,

I'll keep the suffering in.

I take all my wrath out on me,
digging my nails into my skin,
attempting to rip out all my faults,
allowing my guilt to torture and punish me
until I'm bleeding out
and my skin feels like a thousand bee stings.

Satisfied with my penance,
I hide my scars with the sleeves of my jumper,
feeling beaten and worn out,
I crawl into bed and fall asleep.
My slumber reduces my pain
for what a sigh lasts,
I don't want to wake up.

No more anguish please.

Spiralling Down the Rabbit Hole

Down, down,
down into the pit I go,
with my worries
the size of a boulder pulling me in,
the heavy darkness drags me below,

Any glimmer of hope amounts to zero,
no light within,
down, down,
down into the pit I go.

Chaos, anger or woe
befalls in a shattering tailspin,
the heavy darkness drags me below.

I SCREAM!
My desperate voice is the only echo,
the void overwhelms me
resisting the urge to give in,
down, down,
down into the pit I go.

The demons overpower and grow
feeling lonely, weary and unhinged
the heavy darkness drags me below.

Would anyone care if I let go?
No more burden or grief for my friends or kin,

Down, down,
down into the pit I go,
the heavy darkness drags me below.

After Darkness Comes Light

Lonely, secluded in the bottom
of an icy, bleak, gloomy well,
dark waters surround me
threatening to drown me,
utterly fatigued, my energy depleted
from struggling to climb out of the darkness.

I've been trying for so long
to see any gleam of hope or light,
but I feel stuck and stranded alone,
realising I can't get out of this on my own.

I can only whisper "I need help".

I'm afraid…
What if no one comes to help me?
What if they mock me, belittle me,
then leave me by myself again?

No! I have been fighting alone
and it is not working anymore.
I take a deep breath in…
"I need help!" I shout
with all the valour and might I have left.

I hear a voice from above answer,

"I'm here. How can I help?"
I look up, feel the heat
of the sun beam on my face,
it feels like the warm embrace of a mother
soothing her child back to sleep.
I see a hand extended out to me and
for the first time in a while, I smile.

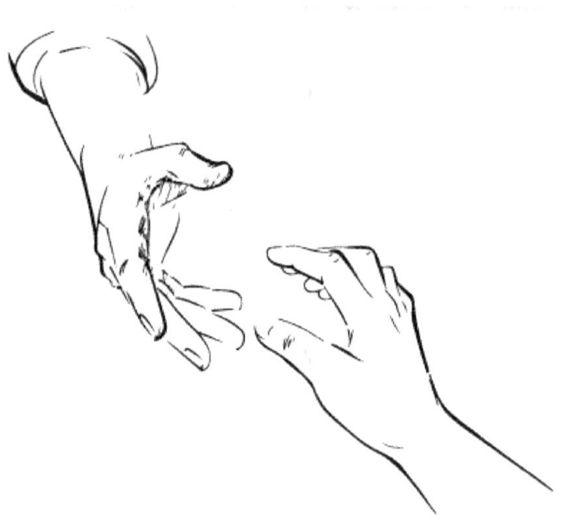

My Support System

I thought I was lost, abandoned, alone,
I thought if I faded away
no one would bother or notice.
I realise now
that I couldn't have been more wrong,
for when I feel lost or in despair,
I have three pillars of support
that I can always lean on for solace and care.

An important pillar is my family,
when my self-worth feels
like it's sunk to the bottom of the ocean,
their belief in me brings me back to shore,
I carry the wise lessons that they teach me,
their unconditional love and trust
inspire me to face the storm,
they are far from perfect,
but they are a perfect fit for me.

Another essential pillar is my friends,
they lend a listening ear
on bad days I need to let out,
when I'm ill or when my demons overtake me
my friends check in on me,
cook my favourite meals and cheer me up,
they are my rock and also my safety net

to catch me when I fall.

The next pillar is the healers of the mind,
they are present in many roles.
When I felt like I was suffocating
I called a helpline,
they are always there,
no compromises, ready to send a life vest.
Then there are counsellors and therapists
who helped me navigate my mind,
developed coping skills using mindfulness
so I don't drown in my emotions.

This is my support system.
In my happiest moments,
they keep me optimistic and joyful,
in my darkest moments,
they are always there to show me the light.

Letting Go and Lightening the Load

I carry a cape of pain and betrayal,
it feels like a ton of bricks on my back,
I cannot wear it any longer,
I must let go to lighten the load.

To the bullies,
I understand now that you didn't hate me,
with daggers in your back,
you didn't know how to deal with your pain
so you took it all out on me.
In the end your torments made me stronger,
more resilient and kind,
you've shown me what I don't want to be,
a spreader of hate.
I forgive you
and free myself from your bitterness.

To my parents,
I forgive you for being too hard on me
or wrapping me in bubble wrap
wanting to protect me,
you were hurt by your own insecurities,
wanting to shield me from any pain,
I know you did your best
and that your heart was in the right place,
thank you for creating a safe home

for me to start my journey,
without your love,
I wouldn't have the courage to be me.

To life,
I forgive you for unfulfilled promises
and rejected dreams,
you taught me many harsh lessons
and took me on rocky roads,
you did not turn out the way I always planned
but you always took me on the journey I needed
to go.
You revealed golden paths to me
that were hidden in the darkness,
I am grateful for the ups and downs
for they made me who I am.

To myself,
I'm sorry and I forgive you,
for all the times I lashed out in anger,
bullied you with hate,
all the regrets, lost opportunities I let pass in fear
and lack of confidence,
allowing it to dictate my life.
I forgive myself for trying to be perfect,
for there's no such thing,
I no longer feel the bricks on my back,
I'm hopeful for the future.
I am at last at peace, for I am free.

Appreciating a Work of Art

As I look upon myself in the mirror,
my mind instinctively splits
into two conflicting voices,
the judgemental critic and the uplifting advocate,
both of them battling in my head
to dictate who conquers my thoughts.

The critic only sees the flaws I have
embarrassed by my tummy rolls
and my big hips,
she tells me I'm useless, a good-for-nothing,
she questions why I deserve to exist.

Then the advocate takes over
and tells me to ignore the negativity,
she helps me embrace my curves
and love my body,
she encourages me to be kind to myself,
allow the goddess within me to be free.

My advocate is right.
I choose to accept my flaws.
There is beauty in imperfection,
I am a work of art.

To create the life I want

I must do the work,
believe in myself no matter what,
others' opinions and paths
will no longer sway me,
my mistakes past, present and future
are no longer an anchor.

I look proudly at myself and say…

I AM enough.

I AM strong.

I AM fearless.

I AM MAGIC.

The Power of Gratitude

Dark, black, and grey
is how I used to see the world,
my soul felt like it was being dragged down
in quicksand by my negative vibes.

Now I see the world in bright colours
and rainbows,
I've learned to see the good in what I have,

While rainy days may come and go,
sunny days are currently here,
with heavy weights on my shoulders now lifted,
I feel as free as a bird,
I could fly so high and touch the sky.

Yesterday it was like I was repellent
to anything that was good,
today I am a magnet
attracting new opportunities and friendships.
When I began to focus on what I gained,
I was instantly thankful for what I had,
this became easier to understand
and accept the challenges before me.

Being grateful opened my eyes
to see the beauty in the universe,

to me the key to happiness seemed so far away,
floating up in space,
now it is here with me,
sitting in the palm of my hand.

With gratitude in my heart,
I am happy to live another day,
and look forward to what possibilities
tomorrow brings.

A Flickering Flame of Hope

A flame flickers in the darkness,
it can be as big as a bonfire
or as small as a candlelight.
This flame is a belief that things will improve,
everything will be alright.

The darkness comes in many forms
to snuff out the light,
rain, wind, thunderstorms and tornadoes,
come to blow out the flame
so the frequency of fear is louder,
life can feel like a maze with no end,
and drag on.

The flame may diminish, hide in the shade
yet it still shines on,
It is important to cherish and feed the flame
so it may never die.
Remember, even in times of darkness,
the sun always comes out tomorrow.

The Value of Happiness

A new house,
a new job,
a new relationship,
how much value of happiness would you put
on these events?

Going for a walk,
cooking dinner,
talking to your mother,
how much value of happiness would you put
on these events?

How do you measure happiness?
We are taught to work hard and grind,
push ourselves past our breaking point
until we are sick, exhausted
and bleeding to death.
Why? So that we generate money,
for only "that can buy you happiness".

Is this the holy grail?

Or maybe happiness is as simple
as a friend's embrace,
seeing a sunrise, witnessing a new day,
or conquering a fear

that no longer holds you back.
How much value of happiness would you put
on these events?

The secret to happiness lies within,
celebrate the big life-changing occasions,
but also be joyful in the everyday occurrences.

Maybe you're not there yet and that's okay,
but if you continue to say yes to happiness,
you can achieve self-assurance and inner peace.